OLLY'S KITCHEN
VOLUME ONE

Best wishes

Alok K. Ray
(OLLY)

ALOK KUMAR RAY
AVIK RAY

Olly's Kitchen Volume One
U.S Edition
Published by Alok Kumar Ray
Copyright © 2015 Alok Kumar Ray
All Rights Reserved

ISBN 978-0-9935501-1-9

TABLE OF CONTENTS

PREFACE 5
ACKNOWLEDGEMENTS 7

APPETIZERS & SNACKS

SAMOSAS (V) 11
ONION BHAJIS (V) 16
NIMKI (V) 19
FISH CHOP 22
CHICKEN PAKORA 27
BEGUNI (V) 30
FISH FRY 33
MEAT CHOP 37

ENTREES

CHICKEN TIKKA 43
RESHMI KEBAB 47
SEEKH KEBAB 50
TANDOORI FISH 53
AFGHANI KEBAB 56

MAIN COURSES

VEGETARIAN DISHES

MUSHROOM AND EGG CURRY (V) 60
MATAR PANEER (V) 63
DIMER DALNA (V) 67

GHUGNI (V) 70

ALOO DUM (V) 74

CHANAR DALNA (V) 77

CHICKEN DISHES

CHICKEN CURRY 81

CHILI CHICKEN 84

CHICKEN KORMA 87

CORIANDER CHICKEN 90

CHICKEN JALFREZI 93

MEAT DISHES

LAMB BIRYANI 98

LAMB DOPIAZA 102

SPICY LAMB CHOPS 106

SEAFOOD AND FISH DISHES

PRAWN MALAI CURRY 110

FISH CURRY 113

ACCOMPANIMENTS

VEGETABLES

ALOO GOBI (V) 117

SAAG BHAJA (V) 120

TARKA DAAL (V) 122

MOONG DAAL (V) 128

BREADS AND RICE

- PILAU RICE WITH PEAS (V) 132
- KHICHDI (V) 135
- CORIANDER RICE (V) 138
- CHAPATIS (V) 141
- NAAN (V) 145
- PARATHA (V) 149
- LUCHIS (V) 152

PICKLES AND SAUCES

- RAITA (V) 157
- TOMATO CHUTNEY (V) 160

DRINKS

- MANGO LASSI (V) 164
- GHOL (V) 166

DESSERTS

- KULFI (V) 170
- KHEER KAMLA (V) 174
- PAYESH (V) 177
- SRIKHAND (V) 180
- SANDESH (V) 183

PREFACE

This first volume of Olly's Kitchen has been written out of my passion for cooking and has been inspired by preparing meals for my dearest friends and family over the past 40 years. As such, this book is prepared with love and each recipe has a personal memory associated with the people I value most in this world.

My journey started in Kolkata, India where growing up as a boy, I got to taste fantastic Indian street food, which has inspired some of the pages in this book.

I am exceptionally grateful to my friends from college who encouraged me to take the leap and move to England in 1968, a decision which I have never looked back at. Whilst by blood I am Indian, England is a country that I love dearly and proudly call home.

Through my love for chemistry I was fortunate enough to work with many talented scientists and designed flavors for companies all over the world. I learned a great many things and traveled to far off places that I had only previously heard of by name. I traveled to a total of 31 countries with my work and the flavors I tasted on those travels have also been fused with traditional Indian recipes to create new taste sensations.

I had the pleasure of cooking Indian food in Johannesburg, Geneva, Bogota, Sao Paolo, Caracas, New York and made many new friends around the world. Cooking in these different places has allowed me to learn about different cultures, an experience, which I can honestly say has enriched my life.

This book is dedicated to my wife, Pranati and my two sons Raoul and Avik. Life has thrown us challenges that we have fought together and which have ultimately made us stronger individually and collectively as a family.

Never stop dreaming and always believe you can make the difference.

Alok Kumar Ray (Olly)

ACKNOWLEDGEMENTS

I have co-written the book with the help of my son Avik Ray who had the vision to turn this dream into a reality and it is one of my life's greatest pleasures to share this experience as father and son.

I would like to thank our photographer Alex Mejia Puentes. We have benefited greatly from Alex's visual interpretation of our family recipes and we hope to be able to show the world that Indian cooking can be simple and appreciated by people from all cultures and backgrounds.

My family has been central to my journey in cooking and those who are no longer with us but have inspired recipes in this book, my thoughts are always with you. Specifically, my elder sister Anima, my mother-in-law Milita and my niece Trina, may you all rest in peace.

I would also like to extend my thanks to my other son Raoul and my wife Pranati who have also continuously provided guidance and improvements on my recipes over the years.

Lastly, I would like to thank you the reader for investing in this book; my hope is that this book brings you and your friends as much joy in meal times as it has for my family and I.

For ease of access and for our vegetarian friends the recipes suitable for vegetarians are noted with (v).

Alok Kumar Ray (Olly)

APPETIZERS & SNACKS

SAMOSAS [V]

Samosas are a deep fried triangular pastry filled with your choice of vegetarian or non vegetarian filling. In this recipe I will show a simple vegetarian Samosa which works very nicely as an afternoon snack or an appetizer for your main course.

Serves: 4

Preparation time: 45 minutes

Cooking time: 30 minutes

Ingredients:

For the pastry

16 ounces of sifted plain white flour

1 teaspoon of salt

6 tablespoons of vegetable oil

4 fl oz of water (note: you may require slightly less, depending on the flour you use)

For the potato filling

2 large potatoes peeled and cut into ½ inch cubes

4 tablespoons of vegetable oil for frying

2 teaspoons of cumin seeds

2 teaspoons cumin seed powder

1 teaspoon of salt

½ teaspoon of dried mango powder (Amchoor)

2 fl oz of water

Vegetable oil for deep frying (the quantity will depend on the vessel you use for cooking)

Instructions:

Pastry

1. Add the sifted flour salt and the oil into a bowl and rub it until you the mixture takes a coarse texture, like breadcrumbs. Add the water slowly and knead into a ball of dough. A little more water may be needed and you will need to check for consistency of the dough.

2. Place the dough on a clean work surface and knead it for 10-15 minutes until it becomes smooth. Place the dough in a plastic bag for half an hour to allow it to rest.

Filling

1. Heat the oil in a large pan, when hot add the cumin seeds and cook for 3 minutes.

2. Add the finely diced potatoes and stir making sure the potatoes do not stick to the pan, add the salt the cumin powder and Amchoor and cook for a further 5 minutes.

3. Add a little water (2 fl oz) and cover. Cook the mixture covered for a further 10 minutes until the potatoes are soft but not mashed. Once cooked, let the potato filling cool down.

Samosas

1. Knead the dough again and divide into 12 equal sized balls. Work with the balls one at a time, rolling into a 5-inch circle and then cut it by slicing down the middle to give you two equal sized pieces.

2. Take one half and seal along the straight edge with water to give you a cone shape. Take the pastry in the cup of your hand and fill with the potato filling.

3. Seal the samosa by overlapping the flap at the top to make a filled triangular shape. Repeat for the other 11 Samosas and allow them to sit for 5 minutes.

4. Heat the oil for deep frying in a karhai on a medium high flame.

5. Once the oil in the karhai is hot, reduce the heat and place the samosas into the hot oil using a utensil such as a slotted spoon.

6. Turn the Samosa repeatedly in the hot oil until they become a light golden colour. Fry all the samosas and keep them warm.

Accompaniments:

Samosas are a great afternoon snack and can be accompanied by tomato, chili or tamarind sauce and a lovely cup of English tea. Once you have fried the samosas, if you wish, you can freeze them for consumption at a later date.

ONION BHAJIS [V]

Onion bhajis are the perfect snack to accompany your afternoon tea, with the savory taste of fried onions, gram flour and the spicy kick of green chilies. Also served as an appetizer to a main meal.

Serves: 4

Preparation time: 20 minutes

Cooking time: 15 minutes

Ingredients:

1 large onion coarsely chopped

1 medium sized potato peeled and grated

1 tablespoon of onion seeds (also called nigella seeds or kalonji seeds)

1 pinch of bicarbonate of soda

1 teaspoon of salt

1 teaspoon of lovage seeds (ajawain)

1 green chili finely chopped

2 tablespoons of chopped cilantro

4 tablespoons of gram flour (if gram flour is not readily available, you can use whole wheat flour as an alternative)

1 tablespoon of water

Vegetable oil for deep frying (the quantity will depend on the vessel you use for cooking)

Instructions:

1. Put the sliced onions, grated potatoes and the other ingredients except the gram flour and water in a bowl and mix well by hand.

2. Add the gram flour and water to this mix and make a thick dough, add more gram flour if necessary.

3. Make balls with the mixture, slightly smaller in size than a golf ball. These are the bhajis.

4. Heat the vegetable oil in a karhai to a medium heat and put the bhajis into the hot oil. Fry the bhajis over a medium heat until they become golden brown in color.

5. Once cooked, serve with a sauce of your choice (chili, tamarind or tomato sauce would be my suggestions)

Accompaniments:

Onion bhajis are often served as starters in Indian restaurants but I think there is nothing better than having a cup of Earl grey tea to accompany these little delights.

NIMKI [V]

Nimki is a mildly spiced savory snack made with fried dough. A moreish treat that you can enjoy with friends over a cup of tea.

Serves: 4

Preparation time: 20 minutes

Cooking time: 30 minutes

Ingredients:

9 ounces of plain white flour

¼ teaspoon of baking soda

1 teaspoon of salt

1 teaspoon of onion seeds (nigella seeds)

2 tablespoons of melted ghee

4 fl oz of water

Vegetable oil for deep frying (the quantity will depend on the vessel you use for cooking)

Instructions:

1. Put the flour in a bowl and add the salt, baking soda, onion seeds and ghee and rub well until the mixture takes a coarse texture, like breadcrumbs.

2. Add the water slowly and mix with the flour to make a dough. Turn the dough over a clean flat surface and knead for 10 minutes until smooth. Allow the dough to rest in a covered bowl for 15 minutes.

3. Divide the dough into 4 equal sized balls. Take one of the balls and roll it out so that it has a thickness of ⅛ inch.

4. Cut the rolled dough into strips and then either diagonally across to make diamond shapes or into small rectangles.

5. Deep fry the dough shapes in hot oil until the nimkis take a golden brown color. Serve hot.

Accompaniments:

A teatime snack that I like to have with a cup of earl grey tea. Nimkis can be stored in an air tight container for later consumption.

FISH CHOP

This is a very popular starter or snack among Bengalis. Although it is called a "chop" it is more commonly known as a rissole in the west. I love the taste sensation of the spiced potato casing in combination with the delicate taste of fish.

Serves: 4

Preparation time: 40 minutes

Cooking time: 15 minutes

Ingredients:

For the potato filling

4 medium sized potato peeled, quartered and boiled for 15 minutes and then mashed coarsely.

1 medium sized onion finely chopped

1 inch piece of ginger peeled and pulped

2 small cloves of garlic peeled and crushed

1 teaspoon of garam masala powder

1 teaspoon of salt

4 tablespoons of vegetable oil

¼ teaspoon of chili (cayenne) powder

For the fish filling

14 ounces of white fish (like haddock or cod) skinned and boiled in salted water for 1 – 2 minutes

1 medium sized onion sliced finely

1 clove of garlic, crushed to a paste

1 inch piece of ginger peeled and pounded to a pulp

1 green chili finely chopped

1 teaspoon of garam masala powder

A handful of sultanas

½ a teaspoon of salt

2 tablespoons of vegetable oil

For the chop batter

3½ ounces of plain white flour

1 large egg (beaten)

7 ounces of fine breadcrumbs

Vegetable oil for deep frying

Instructions:

Potato filling

1. Heat the oil in a pan and fry the onions for 5 minutes until they are golden brown, add the garlic and ginger fry for 1 minute then add the potatoes and salt. Mix well by hand.

2. Add the chilies and garam masala, mix again and let it cool.

Fish filling

1. Fry the sliced onions in hot oil until they become a golden color and add the ginger, garlic, chilies, salt and then add the boiled fish.

2. Sprinkle the garam masala on the mixture, add the sultanas and mix well.

Fish Chop

1. Grease your palm with vegetable oil, take the potato filling in your hand and make a hole in the middle. Fill the hole with the fish filling and make into an oval shape like a rugby ball.

2. Roll the chop in flour first then in the beaten egg. Coat in breadcrumbs.

3. Heat the oil in a deep frying pan and cook it slowly over a medium heat. The coating should be done well otherwise it tends to split while frying.

Accompaniments:

This dish is the perfect starter for a Bengali feast and you can serve with tomato sauce, chili sauce or mustard depending on your preference.

CHICKEN PAKORA [V]

In our household, my kids used to call this "popcorn chicken" due to the size and shape of these mini pakoras. Crispy and spicy, a delicious snack to spice up your afternoon or to share with friends over an aperitif.

Serves: 6-8

Preparation time: 20 minutes

Cooking time: 30 minutes

Ingredients:

18 ounces of skinless, boneless chicken thighs minced

1½ teaspoons of salt

1 tablespoon of fresh ground black pepper

2 medium sized cloves of garlic (crushed)

1½ inch piece of ginger peeled and pounded to paste

2 medium sized green chilies finely chopped

1 large onion finely chopped

1 teaspoon of garam masala powder

2 tablespoons of fresh cilantro coarsely chopped

1 large egg lightly beaten

3½ ounces of gram flour (if you cannot access gram flour easily, you can also use whole wheat flour made from corn which can serve as a substitute here)

Vegetable oil for deep frying (the quantity will depend on the vessel you use for cooking)

Instructions:

1. Put the minced chicken in a bowl and add all the ingredients except the egg, cornflour and oil. Mix well by hand.

2. Add the gram flour (or whole-wheat corn flour) and mix again. Add the egg and mix it thoroughly. Let the mixture rest for a ½ hour.

3. Heat oil in a large karhai or heavy wok. Make small popcorn sized balls with the mixture and when the oil is hot, drop the balls in the hot oil and fry until they are golden brown. Fry as many balls in one batch as the vessel will hold comfortably without overcrowding.

4. When cooked, remove the pakoras from the oil with a slotted spoon and drain the balls on a kitchen towel. Serve hot.

Accompaniments:

You can accompany these pakoras with tomato ketchup or chili sauce for dipping.

BEGUNI [V]

Beguni are slices of eggplant fried in a batter to give you a crisp coating for this delicious vegetarian snack. An Indian style vegetable tempura.

Serves: 4

Preparation time: 10 minutes

Cooking time: 30 minutes

Ingredients:

1 eggplant

7 fl oz of water

3½ ounces of gram flour (plain flour can be used as an alternative, but it tends to absorb more oil)

1 teaspoon of cornflour

1 teaspoon of salt

1 teaspoon of baking powder

½ teaspoon of onion seeds (kalonji seeds)

Vegetable oil for deep frying (the quantity will depend on the vessel you use for cooking)

Instructions:

1. Make the batter by slowly adding the water to the gram flour, cornflour, onion seeds, salt and baking powder until a smooth batter is formed (similar in consistency to that you would use for pancakes). Set aside.

2. Cut the eggplant into circles and then slice down the middle so that you have semi-circle shapes. Dip each one individually in the batter and fry them in hot oil until they become golden brown.

Accompaniments:

A great vegetarian appetizer, typically served alone or with a salad.

FISH FRY

A good solid white fish like Bhetki (Indian fish) is ideal but as you won't be able to find this everywhere, use local alternatives such as cod or haddock.

Serves: 8

Preparation time: 20 minutes

Cooking time: marinate for 2 hours, frying time 30 minutes

Ingredients:

18 ounces of fillet of fish skinned and boned

juice of one freshly squeezed lime

1 medium size onion (sliced)

1 inch piece of ginger

1 teaspoon of salt

2 medium cloves of Garlic

1 green chili

1 teaspoon of garam masala powder

2 tablespoons of cilantro coarsely chopped

flour for dusting

1 large egg lightly beaten

7 ounces of fine breadcrumbs

Vegetable oil for deep frying (the quantity will depend on the vessel you use for cooking)

Instructions:

1. Cut the filleted fish into 4 inch x 2½ inch pieces (approximately) as thinly as possible by cutting the fish at a slight angle.

2. Line the fish pieces in a glass or porcelain tray and sprinkle salt and lime juice over them and allow to rest for 10 minutes.

3. Put all the other ingredients (except the flour, egg and breadcrumbs) in a blender and make a paste. Pour this mixture over the fish and marinate for 2 hours.

4. Take one piece of fish at a time, dust with flour, cover in beaten egg and then with breadcrumbs. Repeat for all of the other pieces.

5. Put all the cooked fish on a plate and cover with cling film. Put the plate in the fridge and allow the cutlets to firm up for half an hour.

6. Heat the vegetable oil on a medium heat in a karhai or a wok. When hot, gently slide the marinated fish pieces one at a time into the hot oil. Fry gently until the fish fry is golden brown on both sides.

Accompaniments:

A green salad of cucumber, onion and tomatoes, a wedge of lime and a mustard sauce. If you are in good company, these also taste great with a glass of Whiskey.

MEAT CHOP

This is a meat based variation of the fish chop and another very popular starter or snack among Bengalis. This time the spiced potato casing is filled with curried minced lamb.

Serves: 6

Preparation time: 40 minutes

Cooking time: 15 minutes

Ingredients:

For the potato filling

4 medium sized potato peeled, quartered and boiled for 15 minutes and then mashed coarsely.

1 medium sized onion finely chopped

1 inch piece of ginger peeled and pulped

2 small cloves of garlic peeled and crushed

1 teaspoon of garam masala powder

1 teaspoon of salt

4 tablespoons of vegetable oil

¼ teaspoon of chili (cayenne) powder

For the meat filling

14 ounces of minced lamb (the leaner the better)

1 medium sized onion sliced finely

1 clove of garlic, crushed to a paste

1 inch piece of ginger peeled and pounded to a pulp

1 green chili finely chopped

1 teaspoon of garam masala powder

a handful of sultanas

½ a teaspoon of salt

2 tablespoons of vegetable oil

For the chop batter

3½ ounces flour

1 large egg beaten

7 ounces of fine breadcrumbs

Vegetable oil for deep frying

Instructions:

Potato filling

1. Heat the oil in a pan and fry the onions for 5 minutes until they become golden brown, add the garlic and ginger fry for 1 minute then add the potatoes and salt and mix well by hand.

2. Add the chilies and garam masala, mix again and let it cool.

Meat filling

1. Fry the sliced onions for 5 minutes in hot oil and add the ginger, garlic, chilies and salt and then add the minced Lamb.

2. Cook gently over a moderate heat stirring for a further 7 minutes.

3. Add 2 fl oz of water and let the mixture simmer until the meat is tender.

4. Reduce the gravy to make the filling as dry as possible without it sticking to the bottom of the pan. If there is excess oil drain it using a sieve.

Meat Chop

1. Take the potato filling in your greased palm and make a hole in the middle. Fill the hole with the meat filling and make into an oval shape like a rugby ball.

2. Roll the chop in flour first then in the beaten egg. Coat in breadcrumbs.

3. Heat the oil in a deep frying pan and cook it slowly over a medium heat. The coating should be done well otherwise it tends to split while frying.

Accompaniments:

As with its cousin the fish chop, this dish is a perfect start for a Bengali feast and you can serve with tomato sauce, chili sauce or mustard depending on your preference.

ENTRÉES

CHICKEN TIKKA

Chicken Tikka is one of my flagship dishes and is always a hit if you have guests over for dinner. A savoury dish made from chicken breast pieces marinated in yoghurt and a blend of spices and then cooked in a hot oven (ideally in a clay oven).

Serves: 4

Preparation time: 15 minutes, marination time minimum 3 hours

Cooking time: 30 minutes

Ingredients:

1.7 pounds of boneless, skinless chicken cut into 2 inch pieces

1 tablespoon of salt

1 tablespoon of powdered white pepper

5 fl oz of plain natural yoghurt

1½ inch piece of ginger skinned and cut into small pieces

4 medium cloves of garlic

½ ounce of kasuri methi (optional)

1 tablespoon of chicken tikka masala powder

1 teaspoon of powdered cumin seeds

1 teaspoon of coriander powder

1 green chili cut into small pieces

¼ teaspoon of turmeric powder

1 teaspoon of garam masala powder

¼ teaspoon of nutmeg powder

¼ teaspoon of mace powder

2 tablespoons of lime juice

2 fl oz of groundnut oil

2 ounces of melted butter

Instructions:

1. Prick the chicken pieces with a fork, rub the salt and white pepper powder onto the chicken in a large bowl and set aside.

2. Place the yoghurt along with the ginger, garlic, chili, all the spices, the lime juice and the groundnut oil into a food processor / blender and blend it to a smooth paste.

3. Take the paste and pour over the chicken pieces ensuing they are coated with the marinade. Cover the bowl with a cling film and leave to marinate, ideally overnight (minimum 3 hours) in a refrigerator.

4. Preheat the grill to 400 degrees Fahrenheit and skewer the chicken pieces on metallic skewers. If these are not

available wooden skewers presoaked in water will also do the trick.

5. Line the skewered chicken on a roasting tin and grill in the oven for 15 – 20 minutes, turning once and basting with the melted butter. Make sure the chicken is cooked thoroughly (the color of the meat should be a golden red/brown color with specks of black). Serve hot.

Accompaniments:

This dry dish can be accompanied with naan bread or boiled rice along with a green salad of lettuce, tomato, cucumber, rings of onion, a squeeze of lime juice and seasoned with salt.

RESHMI KEBAB

A kebab with a soft and creamy texture. I classify this dish in the same family as chicken tikka or afghani kebabs but with a more delicate taste. Marinated in a blend of egg, cheese and spices, when cooked this gives the chicken a lovely soft texture and smooth taste.

Preparation time: 20 minutes

Cooking time: 30 minutes, 3 hours for marination

Serves: 4

Ingredients:

1.3 pounds of chicken breast cut into 2 inch pieces

1½ ounces of mild cheddar cheese (grated)

3 ounces of single cream

1 tablespoon of white pepper powder

1 inch piece of ginger peeled and pounded to a paste

3 medium cloves of garlic crushed

2 green chilies finely chopped

1 large egg

1 tablespoon of cornflour

½ a teaspoon of mace powder

½ a teaspoon of nutmeg powder

1 teaspoon of salt

1 fl oz of vegetable oil for basting

2 tablespoons of freshly chopped cilantro

Instructions:

1. Put the chicken pieces in a large bowl and rub them with the white pepper powder, salt, ginger and garlic paste and set aside to marinate for 20 minutes.

2. In a bowl, use a hand blender mix the egg, cheese, coriander, chilies, cream, cornflour, mace and nutmeg. Pour this mixture over the chicken and leave it to marinate for 3 hours minimum (the longer the better, preferably overnight) in a refrigerator.

3. Skewer the chicken pieces using a metal skewer and line them over a roasting tin. Again, wooden skewers are also a perfectly acceptable alternative. Place in a hot oven at 350 degrees Fahrenheit basting occasionally until the chicken is cooked (when it turns brown at the edges).

Accompaniments:

A smooth kebab you can eat with by peas pilau rice, paratha or naan bread.

SEEKH KEBAB

A traditional kebab made with minced lamb and spices that is best cooked over hot charcoal to get that authentic taste but also delicious when cooked in a traditional oven.

Serves: 4

Preparation time: 20 minutes

Cooking time: 30 minutes

Ingredients:

1 pound of minced lamb (as lean as possible)

1 large onion finely chopped

4 medium cloves garlic peeled and crushed to a paste

1 inch piece of ginger peeled and crushed to a paste

1 large green chili (finely chopped)

1 teaspoon of black pepper powder

1 teaspoon of garam masala powder

1 fl oz of groundnut oil

2 tablespoons of fresh cilantro

1 large egg

1 teaspoon of salt

Instructions:

1. Put the minced meat in a large mixing bowl.

2. Make a paste of the garlic, ginger, chili, black pepper, garam masala with the oil and add to the meat.

3. Add the chopped onions, cilantro, the egg and the salt and mix it well by hand.

4. With the seasoned meat, make cigar shapes of 4 inches x ½ inch wide cigar shapes and roll by hand. I then lay the kebabs on a baking sheet and bake in a hot oven at 375 degrees Fahrenheit for 30 minutes turning as needed.

Accompaniments:

Perfect as an appetizer or a snack. Wrapping this seasoned meat in naan bread with a squeeze of lemon and lime and a green salad makes for a great taste sensation.

TANDOORI FISH

Baked fish in a rich tandoori marinade with a spicy, savory and wholesome taste.

Serves: 4

Preparation time: 15 minutes plus marination time 3 hours

Cooking time: 30 minutes

Ingredients:

4 x ½ pound fillets of white fish (Cod, Haddock, Basa, Hake, Pollack)

juice of 1 lime

1 teaspoon of salt

½ a teaspoon of turmeric powder

1 inch piece of ginger peeled and crushed

3 cloves of garlic peeled and crushed

1 tablespoon of vegetable oil

1 green chili chopped coarsely

1 teaspoon of cumin powder

1 teaspoon of coriander powder

½ a teaspoon of garam masala powder

2 tablespoons of fresh cilantro

1 teaspoon of ajawain seeds

Instructions:

1. Wash the fish thoroughly and pat dry on a kitchen towel

2. Put all the rest of the ingredients in a blender and make a paste.

3. Place the fish in a non-metallic tray and pour the marinade over it. Mix well and keep aside for 3 hours), covered with cling film in a refrigerator.

4. Wrap the fish in baking foil and bake it in a preheated oven at 375 degrees Fahrenheit for 20 minutes.

5. Open up the package and place the fish back in the oven to dry the sauce enough just to coat the fish. Serve hot.

Accompaniments:

A healthy fish dish that you can have with boiled rice and a simple salad.

AFGHANI KEBAB

A chicken kebab with the rich taste of garlic with a cardamom undertone.

Serves: 4

Preparation time: 10 minutes plus 3 hours of marination

Cooking time: 30 minutes

Ingredients:

18 ounces of chicken breast cut into 2 inch pieces

1 tablespoon of white pepper powder

3 large cloves of garlic peeled and crushed

1 green chili chopped coarsely

1 teaspoon of salt

1 teaspoon of powdered cardamom seeds

4 tablespoons of plain natural yoghurt

2 tablespoons of vegetable oil

Instructions:

1. Prick the chicken pieces with a fork and rub them with the salt and white pepper powder and set aside.

2. Mix the ginger, garlic, chilies, cardamom powder, yoghurt and the vegetable oil in a blender to make the marinade.

3. Pour the marinade over the chicken and mix well. Leave it to marinate for 3 hours (preferably overnight), covered with cling film in a refrigerator.

4. Skewer the chicken pieces with metal or wooden skewers and line them over a roasting tin. Place the skewered chicken pieces in a preheated oven (400 degrees Fahrenheit, fan assisted) for 20 minutes, turning halfway. When the chicken starts browning at the edges it is cooked. Make sure it is cooked thoroughly and serve hot.

Accompaniments:

As the dish is quite dry, you might want to have this with some tarka daal along with a naan and a green salad.

MAIN COURSES
VEGETARIAN DISHES

MUSHROOM AND EGG CURRY [V]

An easy to make quick curry with mushrooms and eggs. This dish has the earthy taste of mushrooms with subtle spices. A great vegetarian dish.

Serves: 4

Preparation time: 10 minutes

Cooking time: 30 minutes

Ingredients:

5 ounces of button mushrooms (sliced)

2 medium sized eggs well beaten

1 medium sized onion finely sliced

2 medium green chilies finely chopped

2 small cloves of garlic crushed

½ teaspoon of salt

¼ teaspoon of turmeric powder

1 teaspoon of garam masala powder

4 tablespoons of vegetable oil

Instructions:

1. Heat the vegetable oil in a large saucepan and fry the onions in the hot oil until soft.

2. Add the crushed garlic and the chilies. Fry for 2-3 and add the mushrooms.

3. Season with salt and turmeric powder and mix well.

4. Add the beaten egg and stir vigorously until it is all dispersed within the curry and cook for a further 3 minutes.

5. Finally sprinkle the garam masala on top and give it a quick mix.

Accompaniments:

An easy to make curry that goes well with boiled rice or chapatis.

MATAR PANEER [V]

Cottage cheese and peas in a curry sauce with a rich blend of spices with an emphasis on roasted cumin seeds.

Serves: 4

Preparation time: 15 minutes

Cooking time: 40 minutes

Ingredients:

8 ounces of paneer (purchased or homemade, however you prefer)

1 large onion sliced finely

1 inch piece of ginger peeled and crushed

1 medium sized tomato finely chopped

1 teaspoon of turmeric powder

1 medium sized green chili finely chopped

2 small cloves of garlic peeled and crushed

1 tablespoon of cumin powder

1 tablespoon of coriander powder

1½ teaspoons of garam masala powder

1 teaspoon of salt

3 tablespoons of vegetable oil

3 tablespoons of ghee

15 ounces of frozen green peas

7 fl oz of water

Instructions:

1. Cut the paneer into ½ inch cubes and soak them in cold water with a sprinkle of turmeric powder for 10 minutes. This will keep the paneer soft. Pat dry the paneer using a kitchen towel.

2. Heat the ghee in a frying pan and shallow fry the paneer cubes until they become golden brown on all sides. After frying put them in a bowl of cold water and set aside.

3. Heat the oil in a large pan and fry the onion until they become a light golden brown color. Add the ginger and the garlic and fry for 1 minute. Add the tomatoes, salt, chopped chilies and the rest of the spices and fry together for a further 5 minutes.

4. Add the peas and stir well. Fry for 1-2 minutes. Add 200 ml water and bring the curry to boil. Take out the fried paneer cubes from water pat them dry on a kitchen towel and add to the mix in the pan.

5. Reduce the heat and bring it to a simmer. Cook for 10 minutes, checking that the consistency of the gravy is thick. Boil off any excess water if you think it is necessary. Serve hot.

Accompaniments:

This dish is inspired by our visits to the restaurants of Drummond Street, London where my eldest son studied. To stay true to that experience, I would recommend having this dish with some delicious parathas.

DIMER DALNA [V]

An egg curry from West Bengal. A very simple and easy to prepare vegetarian dish.

Serves: 4

Preparation time: 15 minutes

Cooking time: 20 minutes

Ingredients:

4 large free range eggs hard boiled for 8 minutes (time may vary depending on altitude)

2 medium sized onions sliced finely

3 large cloves of garlic peeled and crushed

1½ inch piece of ginger peeled and crushed

1 medium sized tomato finely chopped

½ teaspoon of turmeric powder

¾ teaspoon of salt

1 medium sized green chili slit down the middle

3 tablespoons of vegetable oil

1 teaspoon of garam masala powder

7 fl oz of water

Instructions:

1. Heat the oil in a large saucepan and fry the onions for 5 minutes until golden. In a separate saucepan, put the eggs to boil for 8 minutes. Note that cooking times may vary, depending on altitude.

2. Add the salt, ginger and garlic and fry together with the onions for 1 minute.

3. Add the rest of the ingredients excluding the water, and fry for a further 7 minutes until all of the spices have blended into a thick gravy.

4. Add the eggs to the gravy, cook for 1 minute and then add water and boil the mixture for a further 5 minutes. Reduce the gravy by cooking on a low heat and check salt for taste.

Accompaniments:

A simple vegetarian curry that can be accompanied with boiled rice, chapatis or parathas.

GHUGNI [V]

Ghugni is a classic vegetarian dish made from curried chick peas which is very popular in my home state of West Bengal. I use a strong blend of spices with emphasis on roasted cumin seeds and coriander to give a delicious taste sensation.

Serves: 8

Preparation time: 10 minutes

Cooking time: 40 minutes

Ingredients:

2 x 14 ounce cans of chickpeas in water (washed and drained)

1 large onion sliced finely

1 inch piece of ginger peeled and pounded

1 medium sized tomato finely chopped

1 teaspoon of turmeric powder

1 medium sized green chili finely chopped

2 small cloves of garlic, finely chopped

1 tablespoon of cumin powder (jeera)

1 tablespoon of coriander powder

1 teaspoon of garam masala powder

1 teaspoon of salt

3 tablespoons of vegetable oil

Instructions:

1. Heat the vegetable oil in a large sauce pan and fry the onions for 10 minutes until they become soft.

2. Add the ginger along with all the other spices and the tomatoes. Fry together for a further 7 minutes and add a little water if the mixture starts to stick to the pan.

3. Add the chick peas and stir well. Fry for 1-2 minutes. Add 10 fl oz of water and bring the mixture to boil for 30-45 minutes in a pressure cooker.

4. Let the chick peas simmer until they become tender.

5. Garnish with your choice of

- finely chopped cucumber

- chopped cilantro

- roasted cumin seeds

- pieces of fresh coconut

- finely chopped red onions

- lemon / lime juice

Accompaniments:

My personal favorite is to have Ghugni wrapped in chapatis or parathas - it takes me back to my childhood of eating from the street vendors in Calcutta (Kolkata as they call it these days!). As an alternative to canned chickpeas, you can also soak 1.3 pounds of dried chickpeas overnight. As they absorb the water, this will give you the equivalent of 2 14 ounce cans.

ALOO DUM [V]

A savory dish of curried potatoes with a thick sauce and a rich flavor. This is a tasty snack but can be enjoyed as a main meal.

Serves: 4

Preparation time: 20 minutes

Cooking time: 20 minutes

Ingredients:

30 medium sized baby potatoes

1 ½ inch piece of ginger peeled and crushed

½ a teaspoon of turmeric powder

1 small green chili pounded

1 teaspoon of coriander powder

1 teaspoon of cumin seed powder (jeera)

1 medium sized tomato chopped finely

3 tablespoons of vegetable oil

1 teaspoon of garam masala powder

2 teaspoons of salt

Instructions:

1. Boil the potatoes for 15 minutes in salted water (1 teaspoon) until soft. Wait for the potatoes to cool, peel and keep to one side.

2. Heat the oil in a large pan and add the ginger, 1 teaspoon of salt and all the spices, fry for 5 minutes until they are all fried and you have a homogeneous mixture. Add a little water (½ a cup), if necessary to avoid the mixture sticking to the pan.

3. Add the boiled potatoes to the curry mix and stir in for 3 minutes.

4. Add 100 ml. of water to make a gravy texture and let it boil for 5 minutes. Check the taste and add more if necessary.

Accompaniments:

This dish is best served with bread based **accompaniments** such as chapatis, parathas or luchis.

CHANAR DALNA [V]

This is a great vegetarian dish with a delicate spiced flavor. Made with cottage cheese (called chana in Bengali or paneer in other parts of India). You can make the paneer yourself or buy it ready made. Instructions to make your own paneer are able in my free to download starter pack or via <u>ollyskitchen.com</u>.

Serves: 4

Preparation time: 10 minutes

Cooking time: 30 minutes

Ingredients:

1 block of paneer (8 ounces) cut into small 1 inch cubes

1 inch piece of ginger peeled and crushed

½ a teaspoon of turmeric powder

1 small green chili pounded

1 teaspoon of coriander powder

1 teaspoon of cumin seed powder (jeera)

1 large potato cut into 1 inch cubes

1 fl oz of plain natural yoghurt

4 tablespoons of vegetable oil

1 teaspoon of garam masala powder

2 tablespoons of ghee (clarified butter)

1 teaspoon of salt

Instructions:

1. Fry the cubed potatoes and cottage cheese (paneer) for 3 minutes and set aside.

2. With a blender, create a paste with the chili, coriander, cumin, ginger, turmeric, natural yoghurt and half a cup of water.

3. Heat oil in the pan and add the paste and reduce by cooking for 7 minutes. When the paste of the spices is fried add a little water (¼ cup) to make a gravy like mixture.

4. Now add the potatoes and cook for a further 7 minutes until the potatoes become soft. When done add the paneer pieces and boil for 10 minutes.

5. Fry the garam masala in ghee for 2 minutes and finish by pouring this onto the mixture.

6. Add the salt and check for taste.

Accompaniments:

As a standalone dish, I recommend you have this with boiled rice or paratha.

MAIN COURSES
CHICKEN DISHES

CHICKEN CURRY

An easy to cook chicken curry, spicy and satisfying.

Serves: 4

Preparation time: 15 minutes

Cooking time: 50 minutes

Ingredients:

4 medium pieces of boneless, skinless thigh portions cut into 1 inch cubes

1 medium sized onion finely sliced

1 inch piece of ginger peeled and crushed

2 medium sized cloves of garlic peeled and crushed

1 teaspoon of turmeric powder

¼ teaspoon of chili powder (cayenne pepper powder) or 1 medium sized green chili coarsely chopped

1 tablespoon of cumin powder

1 tablespoon of coriander powder

1 teaspoon of garam masala powder

1 medium sized tomato coarsely chopped

3 tablespoons of vegetable oil

1 teaspoon of salt

Instructions:

1. Heat the vegetable oil in a heavy saucepan. Add the chopped onions and fry for 5 minutes until they become golden brown.

2. Add the pulped garlic and ginger and fry it with the onions for 1 minute.

3. Add the cubed chicken to the mix and stir on a medium heat for 5 minutes to seal the meat until the meat goes white. Take care that the meat does not stick to the pan.

4. Add all of the remaining spices and salt and keep stir the curry for 5 minutes until the spices have mixed in. Add the chopped tomatoes.

5. Add 7 fl oz of water to the curry to create a gravy sauce and simmer on a low heat for approximately 25 minutes until the chicken is cooked and tender. Continue to cook on low heat to reduce the amount of water to ensure you get a nice thick gravy.

Accompaniments:

As the dish itself is quite rich in taste, a simple accompaniment like boiled rice or chapatis works nicely.

CHILI CHICKEN

As my hometown of Kolkata is close to India's border with China, this curry is a fusion dish of Indian and Chinese Cuisine that has a fresh spicy taste of green capsicum. I accredit to my favorite niece, Trina Sen. In our hearts always.

Serves: 4

Preparation time: 20 minutes

Cooking time: 50 minutes

Ingredients:

8 medium skinless chicken thighs cut into 1 inch pieces

2 tablespoons of cornflour (plus extra if needed to thicken sauce later)

3 tablespoons of soy sauce

½ a teaspoon of salt

1 teaspoon of ground black pepper

1 fl oz of water

1 large egg (beaten)

vegetable oil for deep frying

1 large onion finely sliced

2 green peppers (capsicum) cut into 1 inch pieces

1 green chili coarsely chopped

1 teaspoon of vinegar

Instructions:

1. Boil the chicken pieces in a large pan for 15 minutes. Remove from water and allow the pieces to cool down.

2. Make a paste with the cornflour, 2 tablespoons of soy sauce, salt and pepper and 20 ml of water.

3. Dip the boiled chicken pieces in the paste, then dip in the beaten egg and deep fry them in hot oil.

4. Fry the onion and capsicum in a saucepan, add the chicken pieces and the rest of the soy sauce.

5. Add the chopped green chilies and vinegar and mix together. Add more cornflour if the gravy needs thickening.

Accompaniments:

My recommendation is to accompany this dish with a very simple accompaniment such as boiled rice or boiled noodles.

CHICKEN KORMA

A mild curry with a delicate taste of chicken and almonds and a hint of spice.

Serves: 4

Preparation time: 15 minutes plus 30 minutes for marination

Cooking time: 40 minutes

Ingredients:

2.2 pounds of boneless, skinless chicken thigh pieces

1 teaspoon of salt

1 fl oz of plain natural yoghurt

1 teaspoon of turmeric powder

1 large onion finely sliced

3 medium cloves of garlic crushed

1 inch piece of ginger peeled and crushed

1 green chili, coarsely chopped

2 tablespoons of almond powder

1 teaspoon of garam masala powder

4 tablespoons of vegetable oil

2 tablespoons of chopped cilantro

Instructions:

1. Cut each thigh portion into 1 inch x 1 inch pieces and rub it with the salt, turmeric powder and natural yoghurt and leave it to marinate for a ½ hour.

2. Blend the sliced onion, garlic, ginger, coriander leaves and the green chilies to give you a fine paste.

3. Heat the vegetable oil in a large pan and fry the mixture for 5 minutes, until the oil tends to separate.

4. Add the marinated chicken and stir it in to the paste. Bring the mixture to boil (10 minutes). Cover and simmer for 20 minutes.

5. Sprinkle the garam masala and the almond powder over the top and gently mix it in for 5 minutes.

6. If you like a creamy texture, you can add more yoghurt to the curry. As an alternative to yoghurt, you can also add coconut milk if you prefer a sweeter taste.

Accompaniments:

Great with naan bread or with boiled rice.

CORIANDER CHICKEN

A chicken curry with the full flavor of cilantro.

Serves: 4

Preparation time: 15 minutes

Cooking time: 40 minutes

Ingredients:

18 ounces of boneless, skinless chicken thighs cut into 1 inch cubes

2 medium sized onions finely sliced

1 inch piece of ginger peeled and crushed

3 cloves of garlic peeled and crushed

1 medium sized tomato coarsely chopped

1 teaspoon of salt

1 teaspoon of coriander powder

1 teaspoon of cumin seed powder

½ a teaspoon of turmeric powder

1 teaspoon of garam masala powder

2 green chilies slit in the middle

3½ fl oz of water

10 tablespoons of chopped cilantro

3 tablespoons of vegetable oil

Instructions:

1. Heat the vegetable oil in a large pan and fry the onions until they become golden brown. Add the ginger and garlic and fry for 1 minute.

2. Add the tomatoes and the rest of the spices and salt and keep cooking on a medium heat for a further 5 minutes, stirring occasionally.

3. Add the chicken pieces and cook until the meat seals and has an even coating of the spices. Add the chopped cilantro and the green chilies and mix well. Keep stirring for another 5 minutes. Add water and bring to boil. Reduce heat and let it simmer with a tight lid for 20 minutes.

4. Add more finely chopped coriander and serve hot.

Accompaniments:

This curry is best served with boiled rice or chapatis.

CHICKEN JALFREZI

A spicy variation on the chicken curry for those that like it hot.

Serves: 4

Preparation time: 20 minutes

Cooking time: 40 minutes

Ingredients:

1.3 pounds of boneless, skinless chicken thigh portions (cut into 1 inch pieces)

2 medium sized onions finely chopped

3 medium sized tomatoes coarsely chopped

1 teaspoon of salt

½ a teaspoon of turmeric powder

3 tablespoons of vegetable oil

3 medium sized cloves of garlic (crushed)

1 inch piece of ginger peeled and crushed

1 teaspoon of coriander powder

1 teaspoon of cumin powder

1 teaspoon of garam masala powder

3 green chilies slit in the middle

7 fl oz of water

2 tablespoons of cilantro

1 teaspoon of cayenne pepper powder (optional)

Instructions:

1. Heat the vegetable oil in a large heavy pan and fry the onions in until they become golden brown. Add the ginger and garlic pastes and fry for another 2 minutes.

2. Add the chopped tomatoes and the rest of the spices other than the green chilies. Mix well.

3. Add the chicken pieces and keep stirring for a further 7 minutes until the chicken is well coated with the spices.

4. Add 7 fl oz of water, bring to the boil and add the green chilies. Let the curry boil for another 20 minutes. Cover the pan with a tight lid.

5. Check the curry to taste. For those who like it hot, add the cayenne powder and stir in to the mix.

6. Check the consistency of the gravy so that you have a nice thick sauce.

Accompaniments:

You can serve this with boiled rice or paratha. As it is spicier than the other chicken curries in the book, I also like to serve with raita.

MAIN COURSES
MEAT DISHES

LAMB BIRYANI

This dish is a mixture of slow cooked curried lamb layered with pilau rice and cooked together to give an incredible taste sensation. Credit for this recipe goes to my revered sister-in-law Mrs. Arati Roy of Lucknow; a super cook in her own right.

Serves: 4

Preparation time: 20 minutes

Cooking time: 1 hour

Ingredients:

18 ounces of lamb (preferably from the leg) cut into 2 inch pieces.

2 large onions each cut into 8 even sized pieces

4 - 5 dry red chilies

1 inch piece of ginger peeled and crushed to form a paste

4 medium sized cloves of garlic, peeled and crushed

9 ounces of long grain basmati rice, washed and spread out on a chopping board

4 tablespoons of ghee

1 teaspoon of turmeric powder

2 teaspoons of salt

5 whole cloves

4 green cardamoms

1½ inch stick of cinnamon

1 teaspoon of sugar

25 fl oz of water

Instructions:

1. Put the water in a large pan to boil, add the sliced onion, half of the ginger paste, the garlic paste, turmeric and the red chilies. Add the lamb and also 1 teaspoon of salt.

2. Boil the mixture for 30 minutes until the meat is tender but not totally cooked. Take out the meat pieces from the mix, and strain the liquid and keep to one side - we will use this liquid later to cook the rice. You can discard the residue of onions with other ingredients left in the pan.

3. Fry the meat pieces in ghee for 5 minutes and keep to one side.

4. Use the ghee in the pan to fry the cardamom, cloves and cinnamon (broken into smaller pieces). Add the rest of the ginger paste, the sugar and the rest of the salt to the mix and fry for 1 minute.

5. Add the washed rice to the mixture, taking care that it does not stick to the bottom of the pan. Fry the rice in the mixture for 2 minutes.

6. Now add 17 ounces of the liquid from step (2) to cook the rice. Cook for 10-15 minutes before adding the fried meat into the mix and then stir. Bring the mixture to boil and gently simmer for 10 minutes so that the rice cooks with the meat.

7. Cover the mixture with foil to retain the steam and allow to rest for 2 minutes. More of the liquid may be added if the rice is not fully cooked. The texture at this stage should be al dente.

Accompaniments:

As this dish is a meal in itself, I would typically serve with a green salad of sliced tomatoes, cucumber, onions and chopped lettuce leaves. If you are feeling particularly hungry, you can also accompany this dish with a vegetable curry.

LAMB DOPIAZA

This curry brings out the succulent flavor of tender pieces of lamb in a curry sauce enriched with the flavor of onions. Best results are obtained by slow cooking the meat. As an alternative to slow cooking, a pressure cooker can be used for a faster cooking time.

Serves: 4

Preparation time: 30 minutes

Cooking time: 2 ½ hours

Ingredients:

14 ounces of lamb from leg or shoulder cut into 1-inch pieces (ideally boneless pieces with excess fat removed)

3 large onions finely sliced divided into 2 portions: 1 portion of 2 onions and 1 portion of 1 onion

3 large cloves of garlic crushed

1 inch piece of ginger peeled and pounded to a paste

1 teaspoon of turmeric powder

1 teaspoon of salt

1 teaspoon of garam masala powder

1 teaspoon of coriander powder

1 teaspoon of cumin powder

1 large tomato coarsely chopped

2 tablespoons of natural yoghurt

4 tablespoons of vegetable oil for frying

2 tablespoons of vegetable oil for later use

2 green chilies, slit in the middle

Instructions:

1. Heat the vegetable oil in a heavy casserole pan and fry the slices from 2 onions until they become golden brown. Add the ginger and garlic and fry for 1 minute.

2. Add the meat and fry until it has sealed. Add the tomatoes, yoghurt, salt and all the spices and stir them together. Cook for 20 minutes in the pan.

3. Preheat the oven to 250 degrees Fahrenheit.

4. Make a cartouche with grease proof paper (cutout to fit inside the casserole dish) and use it to cover the meat. Cover the casserole dish with the lid and place it in the oven. Cook for 1 ½ hours at this heat.

5. Take the casserole dish out of the oven and give it a stir to mix. Remove any excess fat from the surface. Once you have done this, check the taste and add more salt if necessary.

6. Fry the slices of the remaining onion in a hot pan until golden brown and then sprinkle it over the cooked lamb curry.

Accompaniments:

A very rich tasting dish, best to accompanied by boiled rice, chapatis or naan.

SPICY LAMB CHOPS

Lamb chops marinated with yoghurt and a blend of spices and baked in the oven.

Serves: 4

Preparation time: 15 minutes plus overnight marination

Cooking time: 1 hour

Ingredients:

4 large lamb chops, excess fat trimmed off.

5 tablespoons of greek style natural yoghurt

1 ½ inch piece of ginger, peeled and pounded to a paste

1 teaspoon of salt

3 large cloves of garlic peeled and crushed

1 teaspoon of cumin powder

1 teaspoon of coriander powder

¼ teaspoon of nutmeg powder

¼ teaspoon of mace powder

1 teaspoon of freshly ground black pepper

1 teaspoon of garam masala powder

2 tablespoons vegetable oil

2 tablespoons of fresh cilantro, coarsely chopped

Instructions:

1. Trim off the excess fat on the chops, wash and pat dry on a kitchen towel and put to one side.

2. Prepare the marinade by blending all of the other ingredients in a blender until it has a smooth consistency.

3. Pour the marinade over the chops and leave it covered with cling film overnight.

4. The following day, arrange the chops in a baking tray, cover with foil and bake it in a preheated oven at 375 degrees Fahrenheit for 1 hour. Check the lamb is tender. Cook for longer if necessary. Serve hot.

Accompaniments:

I like to have these chops with a green salad and some coriander rice.

MAIN COURSES
SEAFOOD AND FISH DISHES

PRAWN MALAI CURRY

This dish is a family favorite and consists of curried prawns in a creamy coconut sauce.

Serves: 4

Preparation time: 30 minutes

Cooking time: 40 minutes

Ingredients:

2.2 pounds of large prawns, peeled, thoroughly washed and deveined.

1 inch piece of ginger peeled and pounded to a paste.

2 large cloves of garlic, peeled and crushed

1 large tomato coarsely chopped

1 tablespoon of turmeric powder

1 teaspoon of salt

14 ounces of tinned coconut milk

2 green chilies (slit in the middle)

1 medium sized onion chopped finely

4 tablespoons of vegetable oil

1 teaspoon of garam masala powder

Instructions:

1. Place the peeled prawns in a non metallic tray and sprinkle ½ a teaspoon of salt and ½ teaspoon of turmeric

powder and rub well so that the prawns are covered. Save ½ a teaspoon of salt and turmeric for later use in the sauce. Set the prawns aside for 15 minutes.

2. Heat the vegetable oil in a pan and fry the prawns gently, turning frequently. Set them aside once again.

3. Leave half of the amount of vegetable oil in the pan. Fry the onions in the oil until they become lightly golden, add the ginger and garlic paste fry for 1 minute and then add the tomatoes.

4. Add half of the coconut milk to the mix and bring to the boil. Add the rest of the salt and turmeric powder (½ a teaspoon of each). Cook for 5 minutes and add the chilies followed by the rest of the coconut milk and the garam masala powder. Keep stirring until a homogeneous mixture is formed.

5. Add the fried prawns and boil in a covered pan for 10 – 15 minutes until the prawns have had time to absorb the sauce. Reduce the gravy on a medium flame to get a thick consistency for your curry.

Accompaniments:

A creamy dish that is well accompanied by plain boiled rice.

FISH CURRY

A simple fish curry using just the natural flavors of green chilies, coriander and onion seeds. I suggest using a fish that does not break up easily such as sea bass, trout, salmon, pollack, bream or grey mullet.

Serves: 4

Preparation time: 20 minutes

Cooking time: 30 minutes

Ingredients:

10½ ounces of fish

4 tablespoons of vegetable oil

¼ teaspoon of onion seeds (kalonji)

2 teaspoons of turmeric powder

1 teaspoon of salt

2 tablespoons of freshly chopped cilantro

7 fl oz of water

2 green chilies slit in the middle

Instructions:

1. Scale and wash the fish thoroughly. Cut into 4 pieces and remove the head (myself, I love the head, but for some people it can be a turn off).

2. Rub the fish pieces with 1 teaspoon of turmeric powder and ½ a teaspoon of salt. Keep aside for 10 minutes.

3. Heat the vegetable oil in a pan and fry the marinated fish gently for 4 minutes. Gently shake off the liquid, taking care not to break the fish pieces. Remove the fish from the pan and keep to one side.

4. In the hot oil add the onion seeds and fry for 2 minutes, add the green chilies, the rest of the salt and turmeric powder, add the water and bring it to boil. Add the fried fish pieces and cook on a low heat until the fish is cooked (10 minutes).

5. I like a thin gravy for this dish. When the fish is cooked sprinkle the cilantro on top.

Accompaniments:

Boiled rice and tarka daal.

ACCOMPANIMENTS
VEGETABLES

ALOO GOBI [V]

The classic vegetarian dish made with potatoes and cauliflower; a great accompaniment for any curry.

Serves: 4

Preparation time: 15 minutes

Cooking time: 30 minutes

Ingredients:

2 large potatoes cut into 1 inch cubes

6 medium sized florets of Cauliflower

1 inch piece of ginger peeled and crushed

1 medium tomato finely chopped

1 medium green chili

½ a teaspoon of turmeric powder

½ a teaspoon of garam masala powder

½ a teaspoon of salt

3 tablespoons of vegetable oil for frying

1 teaspoon of coriander powder

1 teaspoon of cumin seed powder (jeera)

1 cup of water

Instructions:

1. Parboil the chopped potatoes by boiling for 5-10 minutes (depending on altitude) and set aside.

2. Heat the oil in a large saucepan and fry the cauliflower florets gently and set aside. Leave the oil in the pan.

3. In the saucepan, add the pounded ginger to the oil, fry for one minute and add the chopped tomatoes.

4: Add the rest of the spices and fry to get a smooth mixture; add a small amount of water to avoid the mixture sticking in the pan.

5. Add the cauliflower and add 1 cup of water.

6. Add the slit green chili and potatoes. Cover the pan and let it boil for 5 minutes.

7. Heat until the gravy becomes thick. The choice is yours if you wish to let the potatoes and cauliflowers disintegrate, it will give you a different taste sensation compared to if you leave them whole.

Accompaniments:

Delicious as a side dish to your favourite curry or as a standalone main course. It works well with boiled rice, paratha or chapatis.

SAAG BHAJA [V]

This is a typical vegetarian first course from West Bengal and a novel way to prepare spinach.

Serves: 4

Preparation time: 5 minutes

Cooking time: 10 minutes

Ingredients:

18 ounces of spinach

2 tablespoons of vegetable oil for frying

1 tablespoon of butter

1/4 teaspoon of salt

3½ ounces of onion seeds (kalonji)

Instructions:

1. Wash the spinach thoroughly under running cold water.

2. Heat the vegetable oil in a large pan, when hot add the onion seeds and fry for 3 minutes.

3. Add the spinach by handfuls slowly and stir it in until it shrinks.

4. Continue to add until all of the spinach has been added.

5. Stir in the salt and add the butter to finish.

Accompaniments:

A simple dish, best served with boiled rice. For that little extra kick, you can also garnish with some peperoncino.

TARKA DAAL [V]

This is a very popular lentil dish and has numerous variations throughout India. As well as offering a subtle spicy taste, daal is high in protein, high in fiber and low in fat and is popular as an accompaniment or main dish in vegetarian diets.

Serves: 4

Preparation time: 5 minutes

Cooking time: 45 minutes

Ingredients:

5 ounces of red lentils

2 tablespoon of vegetable oil

¾ teaspoon of salt

1 teaspoon of turmeric powder

1 tablespoon of ghee

1 teaspoon of whole cumin seeds

24 fl oz of water

Instructions:

1. Wash the red lentils (daal) in several changes of cold water in a pan until the water runs clear. Leave the daal in the pan.

2. Add 24 fl oz of water to the pan add the salt, oil and turmeric powder and boil for ½ hour on a medium flame until the daal is soft.

The oil is added to emulsify so that the daal does not boil over.

Depending on your preference, at this stage you can use a hand whisk homogenize the daal so that you get a smooth texture if you wish.

3. In a small frying pan heat the ghee and add the cumin seeds until they are gently toasted. Pour this mix over the daal to finish the dish. This last process is called "Tarka" which gives the dish its name.

Accompaniments:

This versatile dish serves as an accompaniment to a wide range of meat and vegetarian dishes. If eaten as a main dish, it goes very nicely with boiled rice or chapatis.

If you do want to have this as a main dish, you can also add vegetables such as potatoes or broccoli to make the dish more wholesome. I like to fry tomatoes with the cumin seeds, but of course this comes down to a matter of choice.

ALOO SHEDDHO [V]

A lightly spiced potato side dish with a chili kick. A classic vegetarian dish from West Bengal.

Serves: 4

Preparation time: 5 minutes

Cooking time: 20 minutes

Ingredients:

2 large potatoes

1 tablespoon of olive oil

½ a teaspoon of mustard powder

1 green chili

1 teaspoon of salt

Instructions:

1. Peel and cut the potatoes into 1 inch pieces.

2. Boil some water with salt and add the potatoes.

3. Boil the potatoes for 10-15 minutes until they become soft.

4. Mash the potatoes in a bowl and add the olive oil and mustard powder.

5. Cut the green chili finely and mix with the potatoes.

6. Check the taste of the mixture and add more salt if necessary.

7. Make medium sized balls from the mix and serve.

Accompaniments:

This dish can be served as a side dish or a light meal. It works well with boiled rice and tarka daal.

MOONG DAAL [V]

This is also another common accompaniment for rice, but the preparation is slightly different to that of tarka daal. This dish has a subtle taste of spices to complement the aroma of the roasted daal.

Serves: 4

Preparation time: 15 minutes

Cooking time: 1 hour

Ingredients:

7 ounces of moong daal (yellow lentils)

2 tablespoons of vegetable oil

1 teaspoon of salt

½ a teaspoon turmeric powder

6 cups of water

Paste made from

1 inch piece ginger peeled and coarsely chopped

1 medium sized tomato chopped

2 tablespoons of chopped cilantro

1 teaspoon of whole cumin seeds (jeera)

½ a teaspoon garam masala powder

1 medium sized green chili coarsely chopped

2 tablespoons of ghee

Instructions:

1. Place the lentils in a dry pan and fry until they become slightly toasted. Wash with cold water and add 6 cups of cold water.

2. Add oil, turmeric and salt and boil for ½ hour or until the daal becomes soft.

3. Homogenise the mixture with a hand whisk.

4. Heat the ghee in a small frying pan, when hot add the cumin seeds followed by the other ingredients for the paste and gently fry to create the paste.

Pour the paste over the boiled lentils and mix thoroughly.

Accompaniments:

As with tarka daal, this dish also serves as an accompaniment to a wide range of meat and vegetarian dishes. As a main dish, it tastes great with just boiled rice or chapatis.

ACCOMPANIMENTS
BREADS AND RICE

PILAU RICE WITH PEAS [V]

A twist on traditional pilau rice with mild spices and the sweet taste of green peas. This dish was a specialty of my elder sister, Anima, who used to make this for us on brother's day (bhai phota) when we were growing up.

Serves: 4

Preparation time: 10 minutes

Cooking time: 15 minutes

Ingredients:

7 ounces of basmati rice

2 inch stick of cinnamon broken into small pieces

4 cloves

4 green cardamom pods slightly split

3 tablespoons of ghee

17 fl oz of water

3½ ounces of frozen green peas

1 teaspoon of salt

1 teaspoon of sugar

2 green chilies split in the middle

Instructions:

1. Wash the rice thoroughly in several changes of water until the water runs clear.

2. Heat the ghee in a large lidded pan and fry the cinnamon, cloves and cardamom for 1 minute. Add the rice and keep stirring until it becomes evenly coated in the ghee mix.

3. Add the salt and the sugar and mix it in and add the water. Bring the rice to boil and at this stage add the chilies and the peas and stir them into the rice.

4. Reduce the heat to gently simmer the rice. Cover the pan with a tight lid (if necessary put aluminium foil and then press the lid on top). Cook it for 9 minutes. Take the rice off the heat and keep covered another 2 minutes. Fluff the rice with a fork and serve.

Accompaniments:

This rice works well with both vegetarian and non-vegetarian curries.

KHICHDI [V]

A mixture of rice and lentils cooked together with a medley of vegetables, subtly spiced. This is a dish I have learnt from my wife, Pranati.

Serves: 4

Preparation time: 20 minutes

Cooking time: 40 minutes

Ingredients:

3½ ounces of basmati rice

3½ ounces of red lentils

1 large onion finely sliced

4 shallots peeled

1 inch piece of ginger peeled and crushed

½ a teaspoon of turmeric powder

8 baby potatoes

4 mini florets of cauliflower

2 ounces of frozen peas

2 large tomatoes quartered

1 teaspoon of salt

1 teaspoon of garam masala powder

27 fl oz of water

2 green chilies split in the middle

3 tablespoons of vegetable oil

2 tablespoons of ghee

Instructions:

1. Wash the rice and lentils in cold water until the water runs clear.

2. Heat the vegetable oil in a large pan. Fry the onions in the hot oil until they become golden followed by the shallots, ginger and the tomatoes. Add the rice and the lentils to the mixture. Fry for 1 minute. Add the salt and turmeric powder and keep stirring.

3. Add the rest of the vegetables followed by the water. Bring the water to boil and then reduce the heat to bring it to a gentle simmer. Cook until the rice is soft and boil off any excess water if necessary.

4. Fry the garam masala in the ghee and stir in to the rice, lentil and vegetable mix. Serve hot.

Accompaniments:

As the dish has a very simple and wholesome flavor, I like to have this with a plain omelet or beguni.

CORIANDER RICE [V]

This rice dish has been inspired by our family in Colombia, I fell in love with this way to prepare rice which tastes great with our Indian food.

Serves: 4

Preparation time: 5 minutes

Cooking time: 35 minutes

Ingredients:

¼ onion, finely sliced

5 ounces of finely chopped cilantro

5 ounces of basmati rice

1 tablespoon of oil

1 quart of water

Instructions:

1. Fry the finely chopped onions in the saucepan with one tablespoon of oil.

2. Add 5 ounces of basmati rice and fry together with the onions for one minute.

3. Add 33 fl oz of water, 1 teaspoon of salt and add the 5 ounces of finely chopped cilantro.

4. Bring the rice to the boil and turn the heat down to a low flame and leave it to boil until the water evaporates. Stir the rice occasionally to ensure the coriander is well distributed in the rice.

5. If you wish, you can garnish with a very small amount of finely chopped coriander to give you an extra kick of fresh and cooked coriander.

Accompaniments:

A great accompaniment to moong daal or tarka daal.

CHAPATIS [V]

This Indian style flat bread is a great accompaniment for both vegetarian and non-vegetarian dishes. The flour used to make this bread (atta) can be found in Indian supermarkets but, if you have difficulty in finding it, you can alternatively use a mix consisting of equal quantities of plain white and whole-wheat flours. Creating perfectly circular chapatis comes with practice!

Serves: 4

Preparation time: 10 minutes

Cooking time: 30 minutes

Ingredients:

9 ounces of chapati flour (or 4½ of ounces plain flour mixed with 4½ of ounces of whole wheat flour as an alternative)

6 fl oz cold water

A pinch of salt

2 tablespoons of vegetable oil

Instructions:

1. Sift the flour and salt through a sieve into a bowl.

2. Add the oil and gently rub into the flour until the mixture takes on the rough texture of breadcrumbs

3. Gently knead the mixture with your fingers, and add the water little by little. The dough should be slightly sticky and will firm up as you continue to knead it.

4. Put the dough onto a flat surface and knead it for a further 7 minutes until it becomes smooth.

5. Place the dough back in the bowl and cover with a damp cloth and leave it for a ½ hour.

6. Divide the dough into 12 equal sized balls. It will be fairly sticky so rub your hand with a little flour when handling it.

7. Dust some plain flour onto a work surface or wooden cutting board. Also dust a rolling pin with plain flour.

8. One by one, take the dough balls and press onto the work surface or chopping board with a generous amount of flour. Roll the dough into a circle shape approximately 5 inches in diameter.

9. Set a heavy based pan to heat over a medium flame and when hot (about 10 minutes) turn the heat to a low flame.

10. One by one, pick up the chapatis and pat them between your hands to shake off extra flour. Place the chapatis on to the hot pan. Let it cook on low heat for 1 minute at this stage the underside should develop white spots due to the heat. Turn the chapatti over with a flat spoon and cook for another 30 seconds on the second side.

11. Take the pan off the stove and put the chapatti itself directly on top of the low flame using a set of tongs. It should puff up within seconds. Turn the chapati over and let the second side sit on the flame for a few seconds.

Cover the chapati with aluminum foil or until all of the chapatis are made.

Accompaniments:

A perfect bread based accompaniment for your vegetarian or non-vegetarian curries. If you are cooking for a smaller number of people, the chapatis can be wrapped up in foil and frozen for consumption at a later date.

NAAN [V]

Naans are flat leavened breads and are popular all over the Middle East and India. There are many variations that one can do, but this recipe covers plain Naan. It is normally cooked in a "Tandoor"(a clay oven) but can equally be baked in a hot domestic oven as well.

Serves: 6

Preparation time: 90 minutes

Cooking time: 30 minutes

Ingredients:

16 ounces of plain white flour

2 teaspoons of castor sugar

2 teaspoons of fast-action yeast

1 teaspoon of salt

¾ teaspoon baking powder

2 tablespoons of melted ghee

7 fl oz of milk (luke warm)

5 tablespoons of plain natural yoghurt

1 large egg beaten

1 ounce of melted butter for brushing

Instructions:

1. Put the milk in a mixing bowl. Add 1 teaspoon of the sugar and the yeast. Stir and create a uniform mixture.

Set the mixture aside for 15 – 20 minutes until the mixture becomes frothy.

2. Sift the flour, salt and baking powder into a separate large bowl using a sieve. Add the remaining 1 teaspoon of sugar, the yeast mixture, 2 tablespoons of melted ghee, the yoghurt and the egg. Mix well to form a dough.

3. Turn the dough out on to a lightly floured work surface or wooden chopping board and knead for 10 minutes or more until smooth. Shape the dough into a ball.

4. Pour a ¼ teaspoon of vegetable oil into a large bowl and roll the ball of dough in the oil. Cover the bowl with cling film and leave it in a warm place. Let it rise for 1 hour until it has doubled in size.

5. Preheat the oven to the 425 degrees Fahrenheit and put the heaviest baking tray (preferably a pizza stone) in the oven.

6. Turn the dough out on to a lightly floured surface and knead once more for about 5 minutes until smooth. Divide the dough into 6 evenly sized pieces.

7. Roll out the first piece of dough into a teardrop shape (10 inches x 5 inches). Remove the hot baking tray from the

oven and slap the naan on to it. Put it immediately into the oven for 3 minutes and you will see it puff up. Turn it over at this stage and cook for another 2 minutes. Brush with melted ghee and cover it in a tea towel. Make all the naans this way and serve hot, taking care not to burn the bread.

Accompaniments:

Naans have a chargrilled flavor and are a particularly good accompaniment to Indian meat dishes and vegetarian curries.

PARATHA [V]

Parathas are a layered Indian flat bread used as an accompaniment to a multitude of curries and also very popular as a snack when served with potatoes or vegetable dishes. This is a personal favorite of mine. If you do not have ghee, you can use vegetable oil as an alternative.

Serves: 4 (16 parathas)

Preparation time: 15 minutes

Cooking time: 30 minutes

Ingredients:

9 ounces of sieved whole-wheat flour

9 ounces of plain flour

½ a teaspoon salt

A pinch of bicarbonate of soda

2 tablespoons of ghee for dough plus one extra tablespoon for cooking.

8 fl oz of cold water

A small bowl of ghee for frying

Instructions:

1. Mix the plain flour and whole-wheat flour with salt, bicarbonate of soda and ghee in a bowl.

2. Rub the mixture with your fingers until the mixture resembles ge texture of coarse breadcrumbs.

3. Slowly add 8 fl oz of cold water and gather the flour together to form a single soft ball of sticky dough.

4. Put the dough on a clean work surface and knead for 10 minutes until a smooth dough is formed which is not sticky.

5. Rub the ball with a little oil and place in a plastic bag for 30 minutes.

6. Make 16 small balls from the dough and dust each ball with flour. Make a circle shape of about 7 inches in diameter, fold it along one side and then fold it again to get a triangular shape. Roll out this triangle so that each side is 8 inches in length. Dust with flour whenever necessary.

7. Set a heavy pan on a medium-low flame.

8. Put the parathas one by one on to the hot pan baking gently and turning frequently so that they cook on both sides. Spread ghee on top of each paratha and cook for 30 seconds. Repeat the process for the other side of each paratha until both sides look golden brown.

Accompaniments:

This flat bread is best served fresh and as an accompaniment to a vegetarian or non-vegetarian curry of your choice. Parathas are also great as a snack by themselves.

LUCHIS [V]

Luchis are a bread like dish popular in West Bengal. I describe luchis as a puffed fried dough with a unique savory taste to accompany Indian meat and vegetable dishes.

Serves: 4

Preparation time: 40 minutes

Cooking time: 30 minutes

Ingredients:

9 ounces of sieved whole-wheat flour

9 ounces of plain flour

½ a teaspoon of salt

2 tablespoons of melted ghee

7 fl oz of cold water

vegetable oil for deep frying

Instructions:

1. Mix the whole-wheat and plain flour along with the salt in a bowl. Rub the ghee into the flour with your fingertips until the mixture resembles coarse breadcrumbs.

2. Slowly add the water and gather the flour to make a soft dough ball, taking care to ensure the dough is not sticky.

3. Place the ball of dough onto a clean work surface and knead for 10 - 12 minutes until the dough is smooth and reform as a ball.

4. Rub the ball with a little oil and place it in a plastic bag and set aside for 30 minutes to keep the dough moist and to let it form.

5. Knead the dough again and divide it into 12 equal sized balls. Work on one ball at a time but keep an eye on the rest of the balls in the bag to ensure that they retain their moisture.

6. Flatten each ball by pressing with your palm onto a clean work surface or wooden chopping board and roll it into a 5 inch circle. It is best to roll the dough out as thin as possible, because it helps the dough to rise when cooking. Depending on how much space you have in your kitchen, all the luchis should be rolled out so that you can fry them one after the other. To preserve the moisture, cover the luchis with cling film.

7. Over a medium flame put enough vegetable oil for deep frying in a karhai and heat the oil to a very high temperature. One by one, take the flattened dough circles and place them carefully over the surface of the hot oil, with a spatula or slotted spoon taking care that you are working with very hot oil. The luchi will most likely sink to the bottom of the karhai but will soon rise in seconds and puff up.

8. Turn the luchi in the oil using a slotted spoon until both sides look slightly golden. Remove the luchi with a slotted spoon and place it in a covered bowl until all of the luchis are done.

Accompaniments:

Luchis are best served hot and are a great accompaniment to any meat or vegetable dish. In our house, we always like to have luchis with aloo bhaja (thinly sliced fried potatoes) or aloo dum.

ACCOMPANIMENTS
PICKLES AND SAUCES

RAITA [V]

Raita is a light yoghurt based relish with a cool and refreshing taste. The medley of yoghurt, cucumber, tomato and onion with a characteristic taste of roasted cumin seeds is a perfect accompaniment to hot curries.

Serves: 4

Preparation time: 10 minutes

Cooking time: -

Ingredients:

17 fl oz of natural yoghurt

10 inch piece of cucumber, peeled and finely chopped

1 large tomato cut into small pieces

1 small onion peeled and finely chopped

1 teaspoon of salt

1 teaspoon of sugar

1 tablespoon of ground roasted cumin seeds

Instructions:

1. Dry roast the cumin seeds and then grind them to a powder using a rolling pin.

2. Put the yoghurt in a bowl and beat it lightly with a fork.

3. Add the onions, cucumber, tomatoes, salt and sugar and mix well.

4. Add the ground roasted cumin seeds mix again and chill in a fridge. Serve cold.

Accompaniments:

I like this as an accompaniment to hot curries like chicken jalfrezi but also has a wonderful taste when eaten with naan bread fresh from the oven.

TOMATO CHUTNEY [V]

A sweet pickle of tomatoes and dried fruits which gives a sweet and sour taste sensation with a hint of spice. A popular dish in West Bengal, especially in the winter when tomatoes are in season.

Serves: 4 to 6 people

Preparation time: 10 minutes

Cooking time: 20 minutes

Ingredients:

14 ounces of tinned tomatoes (chopped)

1 tablespoon of vegetable oil

¼ teaspoon of onion seeds (nigella seeds)

3½ ounces of sugar

1/8 teaspoon of salt

½ ounce of prunes

½ ounce of dates

½ ounce of sultanas

1 inch piece of ginger peeled and finely chopped

juice of ½ a lime or lemon

2 tablespoons of vegetable oil

Instructions:

1. Chop the prunes, dates and sultanas coarsely. Peel the ginger and chop finely into very small pieces (2 mm). Keep these ingredients aside.

2. Heat the vegetable oil in a pan and add the onion seeds. Cook the onion seeds for 2 minutes.

3. Add the tomatoes, salt, sugar, ginger and the dry fruits altogether and keep stirring until the mixture thickens (allow 10 mins).

4. Let the chutney cool down, add the lime juice and stir it in.

Accompaniments:

In West Bengal, this dish is eaten following a main meal with rice, but can also serve as an accompaniment to your curries.

DRINKS

MANGO LASSI [V]

The classic yoghurt based drink with the sweet taste of mangoes.

Serves: 4

Preparation time: 15 minutes

Cooking time: Chill for ½ hour

Ingredients:

25 fl oz of greek style natural yoghurt

pulp of 2 large ripe mangoes (or 7 ounces of tinned mango pulp)

4 tablespoons of sugar

16 cubes of ice

Instructions:

1. If using fresh mangoes then remove the skin and the stones and collect the pulp in a large bowl.

2. Add the yoghurt and the sugar and whisk it using a hand blender.

3. Add the ice cubes and mix them in.

4. Chill in a fridge for ½ hour. Pour in individual glasses and serve cold.

Accompaniments:

This cold drink may be served with your main meal or with other desserts like srikhand. If the lassi is too thick it can be diluted with water to taste.

GHOL [V]

A refreshing drink for a summer's day made with yoghurt and lime juice with a sweet and sour taste.

Serves: 4

Preparation time: 10 minutes

Cooking time: chill for ½ hour

Ingredients:

24 fl oz of greek style natural yoghurt

17 fl oz of water

¼ teaspoon of salt

4 tablespoons of sugar

10 cubes of crushed ice

juice of 1 lime

Instructions:

1. Pour the yoghurt in a bowl, add the sugar, salt and lime juice and whisk it with a hand blender incorporating the water gradually.

2. Add the crushed ice and mix it using a fork.

3. Chill in the fridge for ½ hour

4. Serve cold with more crushed ice and a few leaves of mint on top (optional)

Accompaniments:

No particular accompaniment for this refreshing drink other than good friends and a lovely summer's day!

DESSERTS

KULFI [V]

Kulfi is an Indian style ice cream dessert. This dessert has the rich taste of condensed milk ice cream with the exotic flavor of saffron and pistachio nuts.

I use lidded aluminum tubes (90mm x 45 mm)to put the kulfi in although plastic containers used for making traditional ice lollies can also be used or even an ice cream tub. Note that the preparation of this dessert requires a lot of patience, particularly for reducing the milk. Cooking times can vary depending on altitude.

Serves: 4

Preparation time: 20 minutes

Cooking time: 2-3 hours plus freezing time

Ingredients:

3 quarts of whole milk

10½ ounces of double cream

8 – 10 green cardamom pods wrapped in a small piece of muslin cloth

8 tablespoons of sugar

12 almonds soaked in water, skin removed and then chopped finely

2 ounces of shelled unsalted pistachio nuts soaked in water, with the skin removed and then chopped finely

A few strands of saffron

Instructions:

1. Place the milk in a large pot and start to boil.

2. Tie the muslin bag of cardamom pods to a wooden spoon and use it for stirring the milk.

3. Stir continuously and reduce the milk to 1/3rd of its original volume or when skin starts to form on the milk readily. This is the part of the process where you will require a lot of patience.

Whilst the milk is reducing, you can use the time to also finely chop the pistachios.

4. At the same time as reducing the milk, boil the almonds in water for 5-7 minutes. Allow the almonds to cool down, soak them in water for 5 minutes and chop finely.

5. Once the milk has reduced and has a creamy texture, remove the bundle of cardamom pods and discard. Add a few strands of saffron to the reduced milk and stir in.

6. Add the cream and stir followed by the sugar and almonds. Boil it for just a few more minutes.

7. Pour the mixture in a clean metallic bowl (for good heat transfer) and let it cool to room temperature.

8. Add half of the pistachios and cover the bowl with aluminum foil. If you have one, add a tight fitting lid to the metal container.

9. Put the bowl in a very cold freezer and let it do its work.

10. After 25 minutes, take the bowl out of the freezer and break the ice and homogenize the kulfi. Place the bowl back in the freezer and repeat the process every 20-25 for 2 hours.

11. Cool the containers to be used for the kulfi. Fill with the mixture using a spoon to almost the top and sprinkle with the chopped Pistachio nuts. Put the containers in the freezer and freeze overnight.

Accompaniments:

Served at the end of your meal, so accompanied by digestive of your choice or simply by itself.

KHEER KAMLA [V]

A simple to make but delicious bengali dessert made with milk and oranges. This was one of my favorite sweets growing up in India and credit for this particular recipe goes to my beloved mother in law, Milita Sen.

Serves: 4

Preparation time: 10 minutes

Cooking time: 1 hour (can vary depending on altitude)

Ingredients:

2 quarts of full cream (whole) milk

5 tablespoons of sugar

4 clementines or mandarins, segmented with all skin removed

1 teaspoon of rose water (optional)

1 teaspoon of cornflour

Instructions:

1. Peel and segment the clementines/mandarins, remove the skins from the segments leaving only the small bits of the oranges.

2. Boil the milk in a large heavy pot and reduce it by stirring to get the consistency of single cream. How long you heat the milk for really depends on the altitude you are at. It can take between one and two hours depending on where you live.

3. Add the sugar and stir it in.

4. Add one teaspoon of cornflour to act as a thickening agent and stir in.

5. Cool to room temperature and stir in the rose water (if you are using it).

6. Pour into a bowl and sprinkle the oranges on top.

Accompaniments:

Whilst this is a dessert dish best served chilled, it does also taste very good with luchis.

PAYESH [V]

The Bengali version of rice pudding with a creamy caramel taste, similar to arroz on leche in Latin America.

Serves: 4

Preparation time: 30 minutes

Cooking time: 2 hours

Ingredients:

3 tablespoons of basmati rice

2 quarts of whole milk

5 ounces of sugar

1 ounce of sultanas

Instructions:

1. Wash the rice thoroughly in several changes of water and spread the grains over a clean flat surface to dry.

2. Boil the milk in a large heavy pan and reduce it by a quarter. Depending on your location, this can take between 45 minutes and 2 hours.

3. Add the dried rice and boil until the rice becomes soft, add the sugar and the sultanas and keep boiling until the milk is reduced to half its original volume. Skin will start to form on the milk at this stage. Stir this skin into the mixture and take care that the mixture does not catch the bottom of the pan.

4. Let the dessert stand for a ½ hour to cool down and serve chilled.

Accompaniments:

This dish is served as a dessert and can be served with fresh fruits. Chopped pistachios and almonds can be sprinkled on top to garnish if desired.

SRIKHAND [V]

A dessert made from strained yoghurt and cream with a hint of cardamom and saffron, garnished with chopped pistachio nuts.

Serves: 4

Preparation time: Overnight for straining the yoghurt plus 10 minutes

Cooking time: 20 minutes

Ingredients:

2.2 pounds of greek style thick natural yoghurt

4 ounces of double cream

3½ ounces of caster sugar

2 ounces of raw pistachio nuts soaked in water, with the skin removed and chopped finely.

½ a teaspoon of cardamom seed powder

A few strands of saffron (optional)

Instructions:

1. Wrap the yoghurt in a muslin cloth. Make a loop in the cloth and hang it from a hook. Leave the bag to hang overnight with a bowl underneath to catch the drippings.

2. The following day, soak the pistachios, rub off the skin and chop them finely.

3. Put the strained yoghurt in a bowl. Add the cream and the sugar and blend it with a hand blender until it becomes smooth and fluffy.

4. Add the cardamom powder and mix it well with a fork.

5. Divide into four portions. Garnish with the chopped pistachio nuts and saffron (optional), and chill in a fridge. Serve cold.

Accompaniments:

You can serve with mango pulp or sliced fresh fruits of your choice.

SANDESH [V]

Another typical Bengali sweet made from cottage cheese and perfect for those with a sweet tooth. Sandesh comes in many flavours, shapes and sizes. Making Sandesh is an art form and my home district of West Bengal is famous for it in India.

Serves: 4

Preparation time: 30 minutes plus overnight draining

Cooking time: 20 minutes

Ingredients:

2 quarts of whole milk

juice of 2 fresh limes

6 ounces of white sugar

Instructions:

1. We will be following the same process for making paneer in the first part of this preparation. Heat the milk on a low flame in a large pot until it starts to boil.

2. Once the milk starts to boil and the froth starts to rise, add the lime juice to curdle the milk. Keep stirring for a further minute and allow the curdled milk to stand for a further 5 minutes. You will see that the milk will have cut.

3. Strain the cottage cheese from the mixture using a muslin cloth and a sieve. Put the ball of cottage cheese in a clean muslin cloth and squeeze it to take the water out. The cottage cheese should be drained overnight in the muslin bag by hanging from a hook.

4. The following day, knead the cottage cheese on a wooden board with your hands to get a fine texture. Put

the kneaded cottage cheese in a heavy pan on a very low heat and add the sugar.

5. Stir well and you will see that the sugar will melt. Keep stirring until the whole mass turns into a single solid mixture. This process takes 10 to 15 minutes.

6. Stir for a few more minutes and then pour into a Pyrex dish. Spread it well and score the mixture so that it can be cut into squares. The mixture can also be shaped with molds or shaped into round balls.

Accompaniments:

A typical dessert that can be accompanies with sweetened yoghurt or kheer kamla. You can also garnish your Sandesh with chopped pistachios and dates, the choice is yours.